"...the Lord hears the poor..."

Psalms 69:33

Order this book online at www.trafford.com
or email orders@trafford.com

Most Trafford titles are also available at major online book retailers.

 www.trafford.com

North America & international
toll-free: 844 688 6899 (USA & Canada)
fax: 812 355 4082

Our mission is to efficiently provide the world's finest, most comprehensive book publishing service, enabling every author to experience success. To find out how to publish your book, your way, and have it available worldwide, visit us online at www.trafford.com

Because of the dynamic nature of the Internet, any web addresses or links contained in this book may have changed since publication and may no longer be valid. The views expressed in this work are solely those of the author and do not necessarily reflect the views of the publisher, and the publisher hereby disclaims any responsibility for them.

Any people depicted in stock imagery provided by Getty Images are models,
and such images are being used for illustrative purposes only.
Certain stock imagery © Getty Images.

ISBN: 978-1-4269-6814-3

Print information available on the last page.

Trafford rev. 05/18/2022

Peace in Practice, To the "Non-judgmental" Canadian:

People who say we shouldn't judge people forget that murderers need to go to jail, or that people who perform at work ought to be given raises.

But Jesus said "...judge righteous judgment" (John 7:24 KJ).

When Jesus said "Judge not..." He does not say "do not judge, period." He says, "Judge not, that ye be not judged" (Matthew 7:1). If you tell someone to stop doing something that is wrong, but you do the wrong thing yourself, then you are a hypocrite – and you judge with the judgment of no effect (Matthew 7:2-4). "Thou hypocrite, first cast the beam out of thine own eye; and then thou shalt see clearly to cast out the mote ("speck" NKJ) out of thy brother's eye" (Matthew 7:5). The latter judgment (seeing clearly to cast out the mote) is the type of judgment that is properly effective.

But if you want to live in a perverted world, keep on saying the cliché that we shouldn't judge people.

I doubt you would be happy to be ruled by terrorists.

I doubt you would be happy to have your wallet stolen.

Peace in practice requires judgment.

Be holy (1 Peter 1:15-16 and Proverbs 9:10).

The lukewarm people are seriously warned (see Revelation 3:16).

Blessed are the peacemakers (see Matthew 5:9).

The Good Life and My Understanding

As some people know, I have been writing my thoughts down and dating them for a number of years. Part of this process has resulted in two factory published books: *Advice and Help for Christian Athletes, and Thoughts (Book 3)*. Thoughts (Book 3) seemed to me like it might well be my final book. It seemed quite fitting to end it with the *Letter to Canada*, courtesy of Chris Rice. Thinking there would not be a *Book 4*, I crafted a new invention, a new way to contain my most recent writing – writing which I hope people will find helpful and even more refined in understanding and ideas than my previous writing. The result is the *Postmodern Tablet*, a unique form of combining an old idea into a convenient fold-out. This being created with two pieces of wood, hinges, grey cover stock, ink, and two sheet protectors with the hole punches removed.

In Book 3, I raised a number of concerns, one of the most serious being church leadership (or lack thereof).

Canada, being a western nation, had many founding, Christian-based, laws. To the concern of many, these laws have been threatened or diminished over the past number of decades. A question this raises to any person with conviction is: "what am I to do?"

The laws have become worse. The judges of our land do not appear to understand how to punish criminals, giving them light sentences or brief community work.

Politicians, rather than lead, seem to aim for political correctness.

But worse, is the poor example of leadership in today's local churches. Church leaders should be an example to the state and society. Unfortunately, instead, they are generally slackers who are happy to collect offering monies for their own benefit.

I have my own understanding as to how these problems came about. I point them out precisely in my *Tablet*.

The question, "what am I to do?" is a good one. It takes courage to ask this. It takes self-examination to ask this. Not many, however, self-examine as they should.

The ancient philosophers were bang on when they told us that the unexamined life is the life not to live.

I like to think that the apostle Paul added a great dimension to this necessary self-examination, as he worked with his own hands to provide for his necessities as a humble tentmaker.

Paul was industrious. He did real labor, endured hardship, and was refined.

A leader must be a servant. A leader must have that kind of humility.

The good life is an examined life; for the two greatest commandments *both* involve self-examination (Mark 12:29-31).

I would like to talk about the challenge of being exercised in personal conviction. What happens when things do not seem to be happening well? We need a strong sense of vision to remain inspired. But what is to be done when dreams seem to crumble?

People we might be shutting out of our lives, might be more important than we could imagine. Funny to think of that.

Once we reconnect with these people, new understanding becomes available. New doors can be opened. Opportunities in work and fun are found.

I understand my nature better than ever. I have control over my desires. I understand that I should being working out once or twice a day, six days a week and resting one. My athletic body demands me to work it.

If I am unable to work-out for some reason, I am not alarmed. I now know how to wait on God.

Initiative. Yes. That is also important as well as resting, trusting and waiting. Sometimes opportunities do not come because no direct initiative is taken. Initiate the good.

Enter into the Lord's rest. But remember, the Lord calls all those who *labor* and are heavy laden.

I now have completed work for my own business, obtained through my own initiative.

And I am heavy laden with steel. Go figure, I'm pumping iron I could not budge last year.

Ah yes, the Lord knew what he was taking about. His burden is light. Maybe just like this sheet of paper! But to the laborer our Lord is calling.

Upon the good soil the Lord wants to plant the seed.

Only a ready heart is fit for the Master.

Postmodern Tablet, Side (i).

Possible considerations for those currently attending local churches;

Here are some thoughts for Christians in Nanaimo and Canada (to whom it may concern... or, in other words, "...he that hath an ear, let him hear..."):

What is more important than attending "church?"

Self-examination, energized by divine Love.

-Without self-examination, we potentially cause ourselves damnation (1 Corinthians 11: 27-29 KJ). The Lord wants self-examination, even more than Communion – or attending any "Sunday service," for that matter.

-If we were sufficiently practicing self-examination in this city and in this country; in shameful circumstances, would we be partaking in Communion and offering the sacrifice of praise to our God, in our present, local, "churches?" There are many serious matters, at present, not being dealt with, but rather NEGLECTED. Shouldn't we be asking ourselves the **challenging questions?** Questions like why is there an increasing gap between society and the local "church?" And why are there great drug and substance-abuse problems? And why are so many Christians divorcing? And where is the Recreational Facility/Christian Coffee House, discussed by some, that ought to be open twenty-four hours, seven days a week?

-The "...assembling of ourselves together..." that we are not to forget (Hebrews 10:25 KJ), can evidently take place even in something as simple as a house (1 Corinthians 16:19 KJ). Consequently, the POLITICAL NATURE (i.e. **love of money, abuse of power, and neglect of persons**) in today's alienating local "churches" must be exposed. Christ said, "...my kingdom is not of this world..." (John 18:36). The brotherhood of Christians must be re-established. The sacrificial love for one another, the laying down our lives for one another, must be regained. The early Christians gathered DAILY. They had all things common, eating together, working together... in short, being together happily – without neglect... and without political nonsense.

-The two greatest commandments make NO mention of attending church (Mark 12:29-30).

-Loving God with our whole being involves self-examination. (*Let us ask: what is our whole being*)?

-The second greatest commandment involves *self-examination*, "...as yourself."

-The gap between local "churches" and those outside – those who the Church is supposed to reach, has grown so wide, it is now disturbing. When Christ spoke, "...the common people heard him gladly" (Mark 12:37, my italics). And the apostle spoke of being all things to all men (1 Corinthians 9:22), and practiced this in his LIVELIHOOD, making tents (Acts 18:3). If Paul was asked what he did for a living (to make money), his answer was not: "I am a pastor," or "a priest," or "a bishop," or "a preacher," or "a servant of God." He could answer like an ordinary, **working-class guy**, that he was a "tentmaker."

-The apostle was not without "common knowledge," or what we might call, "street smarts." This kind of knowledge largely comes from experience in working *laboring types of work*, and an awareness of what it takes in life to be able to fend for yourself in a world full of wolves.

-Consider the wolves. Note the nature of a wolf. It is a largely idle creature, like a dog, and crafty in killing prey. Unless it is hunting and killing, it exerts little energy. Like the wolf, so are non-industrious pastors today, who, unrefined (and *unlike* the apostle Paul), ignore trials of **humility**, hardship and impoverishment, and refuse to do REAL LABOR – as they are *inexperienced*, incompetent and as false prophets and wolves (see Matthew 7:15).

-Idleness was a great influencing sin of Sodom (Ezekiel 16:49 KJ). New technologies have caused modern men to sweat less, and consume more - but "...in the sweat of thy face..." was appropriate punishment for Adam (Genesis 3:19 KJ). Physical work and physical activity must be re-emphasized. Idle leaders, *soft-handed leaders, are a* **postmodern crisis**. But change must first begin IN THE CHURCH, before it can properly begin to start in society. Overseers in the CHURCH must be CONVICTED of their CRIMINAL activities (note those of them who commit crime) and forced to pay for their errors and ongoing IDLENESS.

-Society, now, lacks foundation. There is only **one foundation**. This foundation is Christ. Therefore the body (the Church) must become more in-tune with the Head (Christ). The body must MOVE and work and be active and function LIKE IT IS SUPPOSED TO. What is to be made of the inner parts of the body and the bowels of compassion (1 John 3:17 KJ)? What is the INNER MAN? What is WITHIN?

-Jesus said, "...the kingdom of God is within you" (Luke 17:21 NKJ). We should, then, look WITHIN. We should be "*contrite*" or "*conscious-stricken.*"

-Psalms 34:18 KJ "The Lord is nigh unto them that are of a broken heart; And saveth such as be of a *contrite spirit*" (my italics).

-Psalms 51:17 KJ "The sacrifices of God are a broken spirit: a *broken and a contrite heart*, O God, thou wilt not despise" (my italics).

-Isaiah 66:1-2 KJ "Thus saith the Lord, The heaven is my throne and the earth is my footstool: Where is the house that ye build unto me? And where is the place of my rest? 2 For all those *things hath* mine hand made, And all those things have been, saith the Lord: But to this man will I look, even to *him* that is **poor** and of a **contrite spirit**, And trembleth at my word (my bold type).

-Acting as if there are no serious problems is a grave error.

-Amos 5:22-23 KJ "Though ye offer me burnt offerings and meat offerings, I will not accept them: Neither will I regard the peace offerings of your fat beast. 23 Take thou away from me the noise of thy songs; For I will not hear the melody of thy viols."

-We must FACE our problems and not pretend that everything is okay.

-Amos 5:24 KJ **"But let judgment run down as waters, and righteousness as a mighty stream**" (my bold type).

-Hosea 6:6 KJ "For I desired mercy, and not sacrifice; ***and the knowledge of God*** more than burnt offerings" (my bold type and italics).

-Micah 6:1-8.

-Let it be known; any good thing this world enjoys **belongs to God, and to His knowledge, and to Christians,** as the heathen and profane (non-Christian and non-religious) persons have no lawful possession (St. Augustine). Christians must take back the Good and Truth that is rightfully theirs.

-Let us, then, truly and seriously SELF-EXAMINE, and stop the denial and ignorance of real, ongoing, problems.

Postmodern Tablet, Side (ii).

December 18, 2009
-Fasting, lamenting, listening to music which brings back good memories – these things can help bring purpose to present situations. Thank-you Lord. Amen.

November 1, 2009
-**Profane logic** is a cause of great ills. There is no such thing as "blind faith."

October 23, 2009
-Christianity and Human Experience
-Two Great Laws
-The Problem of Neglect
-Christian Dialogue
-Spiritual Deprivation

October 2, 2009
-A Troubled Church; A Troubled Society.
-A Troubled Society; Understanding the Issue.

September, 2009
-No notes.

August, 2009
-No notes

July 16, 2009
-Right exercise not only changes your body – it changes your mind.
-Right exercise is like a vaccination for adversity.

June 21, 2009
-Weak or strong, there is no respect of persons with God. "...All have sinned..." (Romans 3:23 KJ). *Some love mercy*, others don't. ("He hath shewed thee, O man, what is good; and what doth the LORD require of thee, but to do justly, and to love mercy, and to walk humbly with thy God" Micah 6:8, my italics)? People in need (even David, a *king*, called himself "poor" and "needy") find mercy with God, because they seek it. They draw near to God.

June 14, 2009
-Notice how powerless people seem to be, and hope in God's mercy. Revelation 3 says: 17 "Because thou sayest. 'I am rich, and increased with goods, and have need of nothing;' and knowest not that art wretched, and miserable, and poor, and blind, and naked: 18 I counsel thee to buy of me gold tried in the fire, that thou mayest be rich; and white raiment, that thou mayest be clothed, and that the shame of thy nakedness do not appear; and anoint thine eyes with eye-salve, that thou mayest see."
-Become powerful by the mercies of God (Romans 12).

May 21, 2009
-Lament patiently.

May 16, 2009
-Friendship Vision
-Value, empowerment, fun.
-Friendship Telos*
-Friendship moving towards the True Goal (Christ-like care... sacrificial love). "Greater love hath no man than this, that a man lay down his life for his friends" John 15:13 KJ.

April 15, 2009
-The Importance of Sight.
-Vision.
-"The light of... the eye...", what Jesus said (read Matthew 6:22-23).
-Maintain and *uphold* sight. Behold!
-Moses (with a good view) held up the rod and Israel won the battle (Exodus 17:8-16).
-Paul's heavenly vision. The impact it had.
-In Revelation 3:18 sight is a key component.
-Goal setting? *Goals cannot be properly set without vision.*
-"Where there is no vision the people perish..." Proverbs 29:18 (KJ).

March 10, 2009
-Know and respect that the NUMBER ONE is a key number in the first commandment of loving the Lord your God.
-Deuteronomy 6: 4 "Hear, O Israel: The LORD our God is one LORD:" (my highlight) 5 "And thou shalt love the LORD thy God with all thine heart, and with all thy soul, and with all thy might." 6 "And these words, which I command thee this day, **shall be in thine heart:**" (KJ) (my highlight).
-"*One does not come from many, but many from one...*" St. Augustine (my italics).
-The meaning and impact of One is huge: distinct, set apart, individual, undivided, uncommon, just, singleness of heart, made whole, simple, united, balanced, pure, collective, singular, respect, love, justice...

*On the Greek word "Telos" (in other words, "End Goal"):

Everything is moving towards a goal. It is our job to understand what it is, and what it means to each one of us personally. "Know thyself" is something Plato wrote. Aristotle expanded on this, and talked about "first causes," implying that God is ultimately the Cause of causes, but everything has within its nature specific elements that makes things what they are (eg. a dandelion has distinctions that make it dandelion). Individually, this can be useful in understanding your identity - what really makes you, you. Example: I am a man, sweat and physical work is an important part of my nature and fits with the way my muscles are (different composition than a woman's). Men, then, should find a level of distinct happiness when they respect physical work and common labor, and resolve to embrace their masculinity and physicality.

Notes:

February 23, 2002
-Why should society and culture be respected? In order to be effectively supportive of people, society and culture must be appreciated and better understood.
-For those who have no interest in Christianity, what are the most positive things in society? What things of our society influence people positively, whether they are Christians or not?
-Apart from things that you must do, what activities do you feel influence you and your society most positively?
-What things do you feel especially influence society and culture in a positive way?

November 16, 2002
-Becoming a distinguished person means becoming a pure and a consistent person.

Date Unknown
-Heart, communicate, assemble, teach, prosper; think, interact, respect, educate, produce.
-Having enough rest is important.
-There is something special about freeing people in their thinking.
-Enter into something gracefully and get out of it gracefully: essays, eating, a day.

Date Unknown
-"We have developed technologies before we had the wisdom."

Date Unknown
-Treating people as if they have something to offer until they actually do offer something helps to instil confidence in them.

March 28, 2004
-If your story is worthwhile, it is more important to get your story out than to make money. So agree to some kind of terms with a publisher.

November 19, 2004
-The need to be taken seriously.

January 16, 2005
-Holiness is priority. Purity is beauty, and this beauty is highly desirable.

January 24, 2005
-Bitterness is anger without intent. My anger has intent, and my intent is positive.

February 14, 2005
-Father, God: I ask that I will know your love, so that I can be confident and at peace.

February 24, 2005
-The False Innocence of Contemporary Times

March 4, 2005
-The Power to Overcome
-I believe, I have received; now I wish to give. I want to make people believe.
-People must not get hung up on historical analysis, psychological explanations, humanistic reasoning, sociology, evolution, geography, biology, science, or even the Bible (in a misinterpreting way).
-False innocence: excusing ourselves, perverted psychology, applauding injustice, reaction instead of action.
-How People Respond
-How people respond shows how they have chosen to express themselves. The most common way people do this is through conversation, although people's expressions are especially emphasized in song, writing, sport, and art. If people do not have at least one kind of creative activity in their lives that they truly look forward to, and can openly express, their lives are in danger, to some extent, and they will respond poorly to whatever flies in their face – be it good or evil.
-The Grounds of Christian Unification
-What is at stake is genuine Christian fellowship. There needs to be some kind of local environment that allows Christians consistent fellowship that is not restrained and not limited to a pastor's time or timetable. This would be true fellowship, because it would not be under false, man-made, authority. No man would acceptably impose himself.

March 15, 2005
-Spiritual responses are powerful ones.

March 22, 2005
-Spiritual matters "airy?" No. They are pure and vital air, without which people suffocate.
-Hold Your Ground
-The Keeping of Your Soul
-Excusing Ourselves (same-sex marriage, light criminal sentencing, adultery, abortion).
-How We Excuse Ourselves

September 26, 2005
-Corporate Christianity is impossible. "You cannot serve God and mammon."

December 2, 2006
-Why would God pay more attention to people if they fast? I think because of their respect. It is the respect factor (not always the fasting or dead works).

August 8, 2008
-The Lessons of History: it is not that God needed to have more of an understanding of people; but rather, that people needed to have more of an understanding of God. People could not handle too much at once.

<u>Thoughts (Book 3)</u> by Malcolm Rae, now available online through Amazon.com and Malcolm's Publishing (contact: malspaint@gmail.com), is also now released by Trafford Publishing (www.trafford.com).

About the Author:

Malcolm Rae has a diploma in Physical Education and a Bachelor of Arts with a Liberal Studies Major from Malaspina University College (now Vancouver Island University). He has played hockey in Winnipeg, for the Canadian Mennonite University. Rae is also an experienced house painter.

About the Book:

This book contains thoughts in a chronological manner while providing the reader with different options in how they wish to read the text. The underlining, the italics, the bold type, the capitalized words, offer contemplative analysis of justice and contemporary experience. After reading the book cover to cover (due to its time-sequenced nature, it is recommended that the book is read in one sitting) the reader may choose to read only the words that are underlined, or the bold words, or the italicized words, and so forth. The words that are underlined are potential titles for future books. The charcoal artwork, on page five, and the "Letter to Canada," on page fifty-five, are by Christopher R. Rice.

*Note on charcoal artwork: "It's an angel granted power during the end of time, and the scales represent the scales of God's truth, weighing the righteous intent of each man against his unrighteous intent." – Christopher R. Rice

<u>"Messianic-friendly" Prayers</u>:

Before eating:

"Blessed are You, Lord our God. Hallowed be Your name. You are King of the Universe, You created all things by Your Word. Blessed are You, Lord our God, You bring forth bread from the earth. We thank You, Lord our God, for this food. Amen."

After eating:

"Blessed are You, Lord our God. You are glorified now and forever. We thank You for Your mercies, and we remember the Lord's prayer:

(Recite the Lord's prayer, Matthew 6:9-13).

We acknowledge You, Heavenly Father, in the name of Jesus, who is both the Messiah of the Jews and the Savior of the whole world. Amen.

<u>Faith at Work and the Title of This Book</u>

If we are to "fight the good fight of faith…", as if a battle is really going on, shouldn't we be *training* a bit like WARRIORS (1 Timothy 6:12)? Please note that the Bible does not record all of the things which Jesus did (John 21:25). The Bible, therefore, has omissions of some good information. We should recognize, then, that there are some good things that are not actually found in the Bible. What is to be made of this?

Although the reality may be frightening to some (especially to those who do not labor with callused hands ("…the laborers are few…" Luke 10:2), and also to those who despise the working, just, poor), it does present the contrite and industrious believer a real invitation.

Here is my own understanding:

The good, yet omitted, information not found in the Bible can be, in faith, compensated for, by living a godly, contrite, lifestyle. Therefore, let it be known to the inexperienced, non-laboring, non-examining, Christian, that **righteousness is something to be "wrought" ("worked" NKJ, Hebrews 11:32 KJ).** There is a list of individuals in Hebrews 11 who lacked our Scripture, yet they were counted as righteous. The works of these individuals (their works are listed in detail) show proof of their faith. They, in faith, "wrought" or "worked" righteousness… and so should we. We need to have *faith that is evident.*

BATTLE! This is a motivating *key word* – for anyone who does, indeed, care.